50 Billion Reasons to Grow Your Practice

Very Best to you Matt!

Very Best
to you
Matt!

50 Billion Reasons to Grow Your Practice

A GUIDE TO SUCCESS & ENJOYMENT FOR INVESTMENT ADVISORS

Robert A. DiMeo

FOREWORD BY THOMAS J. ANDERSON
NEW YORK TIMES BEST-SELLING
AUTHOR OF *THE VALUE OF DEBT*

ISBN: 0692788662
ISBN 13: 9780692788660
Library of Congress Control Number: 2016916345
Honor Publishing, Chicago, IL

This book is dedicated to my immensely talented business partners and associates who helped build our firm; to my family and especially my sons, Chris and Danny, who generate great joy in my life; to my loving wife, Terri, who beyond her love and support is the wisest woman I know; and to God for His countless teachings and blessings. Also, my deepest appreciation goes to Tom Anderson for contributing the foreword.

This book is intended to provide practice management and other relevant information to investment professionals. The concepts and strategies presented do not in any manner represent investment recommendations. Any reference to investment performance is generic in nature. Past performance does not guarantee future results. Information is obtained from a variety of sources believed, though not guaranteed, to be accurate.

Contents

Foreword by Thomas J. Anderson

In the year 2000, I was just starting out as a financial advisor when I had a meeting with a client who voiced some concerns. The client had seen others benefit extensively from the tech boom of the late '90s, and felt as if they were missing out. My client wanted to be part of the wave. They wanted more tech stocks in their portfolio. So what did I say? "Of course!"

You likely know what happened next. The boom was soon followed by a big bust. My client was understandably upset and left. He wanted brown shoes, so I sold him brown shoes.

Around that time, I began to follow Bob DiMeo's career and have been lucky in getting to know him personally over the past few years. He has become a close friend and trusted mentor, helping me understand the importance of having a process. In this book, Bob provides a firsthand example of a client wanting brown shoes and how he took an approach opposite to mine.

The experience with that particular client has always stuck with me. I have learned from people like Bob over the years and have become inspired to develop my own process. In my years working with other advisors, I have heard (over and over again) about their perpetual desire for a simple guide, a road map, of things to know and do to become better advisors. Traditionally, I would refer advisors to several books. Each had a few great concepts, but the advisors certainly had to work hard to separate the wheat from the chaff.

Now, you and I have the opportunity to learn from one of the best teachers for building an investment consulting business. In this book, Bob shares the playbook that has brought him a career of remarkable success. Whether you have been in the business for eighteen months or eighteen years, he narrows the focus to key concepts that are pivotal in both your practice and your life. The foundational pillars presented on leadership, practice management, hiring and managing, marketing, investing, and life balance represent core fundamentals that every advisor needs to focus on daily. Within these pillars, he frames a subseries of concepts that are essential to new and experienced advisors alike.

While some ideas are important reminders, others represent nuanced lessons. As you encounter this book, I encourage you to stop, think, and reflect on the messages you are receiving—they come from someone who began a business with almost nothing that currently advises on more than $60 billion in assets.

Embracing these ideas has worked for me. I am confident they can work for you as well. I have learned from my friend and mentor. I learned not to sell brown shoes, and my practice took off when Bob taught me differently. And if you're wondering what happened to the client to whom I sold brown shoes...they went to Bob DiMeo.

Preface: Why I Wrote This Book and How to Use It

The fall of 2013 had me traveling on business. Shortly before heading to a meeting, I remember my participation in a call with the CEO and also the COO of a high-quality, midsize investment advisory firm. Some fifteen years earlier, the COO had engaged DiMeo Schneider as the "research engine" for the advisory division that he ran at a large broker-dealer. On that particular day, the two simply sought my perspective on a few practice management topics, including hiring, partnerships, and succession. I looked forward to helping out.

What happened at the beginning of our conversation was both surprising and somewhat awkward. Before we delved into the agenda, the CEO took what seemed like an uncomfortable amount of time to thank me and praise me for my contributions to the profession. Apparently, he had followed our firm's growth over the years, and he might have attended some of my speaking engagements (I served on IMCA's board and chaired the Practice Management effort). His compliments were flattering. I thanked him and quickly pointed out that none of this would have been possible without a large number of very talented partners and colleagues who are professionally aligned and thoughtfully driven. His praise was flattering, though I quickly nudged the conversation toward our agenda.

The following week, our head of marketing notified me that DiMeo Schneider had just crossed the $50 billion threshold in assets under advisement. I tend not to dwell on success, preferring to count my blessings and endeavor forward, but this was a bit of a "Wow!" moment—a symbol of attainment representing the culmination of immense effort by so many caring and skilled colleagues, in addition to healthy doses of great clients and good fortune. Perhaps the combination of the glowing compliments the prior week and then this milestone achievement overwhelmed me. Perhaps something else had happened. Whatever it was inspired a deep sense of gratitude in me—I decided that day that I would write this book, and I even coined the title on the spot.

It's worth sharing that no one, including me, has mastered or will ever completely master managing an investment advisory practice. Markets change, people change, technology advances, and firms evolve. And advisors like you bring a lot to the table. In fact, your interest in this subject in and of itself likely marks you as above average in your profession, and I'd welcome the opportunity to benefit from your knowledge.

I've been the managing director at the firm since its inception in 1995, though I also work directly with clients, as do many of my partners. Throughout my career, I've been blessed to advise some of the largest professional service organizations in the world, including exceptional law firms and architectural firms. It's as though I've been on a twenty-five-year tutorial, and it really feeds my hunger to constantly improve and advance the ways in which we do things. I imagine you also strive to make both your practice and your life more successful. If so, I believe you'll enjoy this book.

Please allow me to provide some insight on the book's title, because it risks coming off as boastful. Candidly, I think "50 billion" is a bit catchy, though the message is absolutely not about measuring success by counting your money; it's about creating something that can endure, add value (for clients and colleagues), and provide you enjoyment and fulfillment.

How to Use This Book

While the book addresses six essential components for success and enjoyment in managing an investment advisory practice, it does so in an asymmetrical fashion. Some sections and chapters are "quick hits" intended to introduce certain concepts for your benefit. Other topics merit and require more detail, and these are the lengthier sections. You'll learn some of the content for the first time, and you'll also receive important reminders of the things we already know but should practice more often. Most important, it's all packaged in user-friendly fashion. Read it cover to cover or leap right to the sections that you find most pressing.

It's my sincere hope that this book helps you enhance your practice and adds enjoyment to your life. It's also my hope that you "pay it forward" in the way you manage, mentor, and guide those you touch.

PART I

Leadership

CHAPTER 1

Leadership Is a Privilege

> Leadership is not magnetic personality. That can just as well be a glib tongue. It is not making friends and influencing people: that is flattery. Leadership is lifting a person's vision to higher sights, the raising of a person's performance to higher standards, the building of a personality beyond its normal limitations.
>
> —Peter Drucker

⅄ ⅄ ⅄

If you're responsible for leading an advisory practice or a team within one, consider yourself blessed. Yes, certain duties and responsibilities seem overwhelming at times, but remember that leaders have the opportunity to profoundly impact the lives of those on their team along with the lives of many others.

We're not placed in leadership roles to respond to "stuff" all day. Leaders advance people, departments, and organizations. In the chapters ahead, we'll examine many qualities and practices that make leaders great; however, it's worth noting here that one of the most essential values in leadership is optimism—no one wants to follow a negative leader. What's more, great leaders also express humility, which can be demonstrated by their ongoing quest to learn (as you are doing by reading this book). And great leaders possess willpower or grit far exceeding that of an everyday person.

Former Secretary of State Condoleezza Rice elegantly described extraordinary leaders in the following manner:

> A true leader never accepts the world as it is but strives always to make the world as it should be. An effective leader must have a clear idea of where they are trying to lead the team or organization that they are leading. They will be willing to take risks and selfless action in order to reach this vision, which will inspire others to do the same.

Thoughts

Leaders clearly see their visions for the future and, at times, become frustrated when others don't enthusiastically embrace those visions. Remember that change is difficult for most people. Sometimes you can more effectively communicate your vision for the future if you first drive home the reasons why current practices are doomed. It's a sequencing thing—that is, the people you lead will be more open to your vision if they first understand the dangers of status quo.

CHAPTER 2

Growth Is Not Optional

> The answer is economic growth isn't just about more stuff. Growth is different from consumerism. Growth is really about the capacity of a nation to produce everything that's wanted and needed by its inhabitants. That includes better stewardship.
>
> —Robert Reich, chancellor's professor of public policy at UC Berkeley

⅄ ⅄ ⅄

At DiMeo Schneider, we do not view growth as optional; in fact, it's a requirement in our strategic plan but perhaps for less than obvious reasons.

While all companies must remain profitable to endure, additional profits are not the primary purpose of our mandated growth. Growth is essential at our firm for two reasons:

1. **Professional Satisfaction.** We are a people business and our "assets" go up and down the elevator each day.

Without smart, positive, caring professionals, we wouldn't have a business. Our growth has enabled us to recruit, retain, reward, and—perhaps most important—stimulate truly unique and talented colleagues.

2. **Acts of Service.** We realize that DiMeo Schneider will never be mistaken as a charitable organization or community foundation; however, we absolutely revere our role in assisting clients. Our people take pride in the fact that our efforts and advice directly benefit hundreds of thousands of retirement-plan participants, students, patients, families, and others.

Thoughts

Growth can be hard work, but it's also exciting and fun. And for us, it's the only way.

CHAPTER 3

A Healthy Organization: The Only Remaining Competitive Advantage

All the competitive advantages we've been pursuing during our careers are gone.

That's right. Strategy. Technology. Finance. Marketing. Gone. No, those disciplines have not disappeared. They are all alive and well in most organizations. And that's good, because they're important. But as meaningful competitive advantages, as real differentiators that can set one company apart from another, they are no longer anything close to what they once were.

That's because virtually every organization, of any size, has access to the best thinking and practices around strategy, technology and those other topics. In this age of

> the internet, as information has become ubiquitous, it's almost impossible to sustain an advantage based on intellectual ideas.
>
> However, there is one remaining, untapped competitive advantage out there, and it's more important than all the others ever were. It is simple, reliable and virtually free. What I'm talking about is organizational health.
>
> —Patrick Lencioni, author of 10 business books and founder of The Table Group

▲ ▲ ▲

Do you still believe you can outwork and outsmart the competition? I did early in my career, but then I ultimately realized that working hard and being smart are mere entry stakes in business. Any average or solid company has smart, hardworking people. That's why Patrick Lencioni's message resonated so strongly when I first heard him speak. I couldn't agree more when he declared that effort and intellect are fleeting advantages—competitors always catch up.

So how can you develop a lasting competitive advantage? By creating a *healthy organization*. Yes, there's a good amount that goes into doing so, but a healthy organization is an entity that has essentially eliminated politics, confusion, and poor morale from its environment. In a healthy organization, productivity soars, and good people don't leave. Leadership is focused (if everything is important then nothing is), communicative, disciplined, and courageous.

And if you're starting to think this sounds rather touchy-feely or if you as a leader are more motivated by the "stuff that matters," let me strongly caution you. This is tangible and practical and as important, actually more important, as any business practice. You see, there are countless examples of smart organizations—ones that have mastered strategy, finance, marketing, or technology—that fail because they're unhealthy. But healthy organizations find a way to succeed. The absence of politics and confusion enables them to become smarter continuously and to tap into all of their intelligence and talent.

This approach may not work for you if you're into sexy schemes or if you're fueled by crisis management. But if you're committed to enduring success, it's imperative to trust that a healthy organization is your only competitive advantage.

Lencioni identifies four simple yet challenging steps that produce healthy organizations:

1. Build a Cohesive Team
2. Create Clarity
3. Over Communicate Clarity
4. Reinforce Clarity

Resources

The Four Obsessions of an Extraordinary Executive, by Patrick Lencioni

The Advantage: Why Organizational Health Trumps Everything Else in Business, by Patrick Lencioni

"Guideposts for Hiring," chapter 17 of this book

CHAPTER 4

The Illusion of Knowledge

> The greatest enemy of knowledge is not
> ignorance; it is the illusion of knowledge.
> —Stephen Hawking

⅄ ⅄ ⅄

Knowledge is powerful and crucial in an advisor's quest to build a successful practice. That you're reading this book implies that you regularly pursue opportunities to increase your knowledge. However, sometimes it's possible to get caught up in what we *know*, and doing so can lead to a narrow perspective—one that negatively impacts our behavior and future decisions.

Knowledge is a good thing...unless it leads to rigidity and a dismissal of additional learning. Allow me to share one widely quoted statistic as an illustration. Official data says that the US unemployment rate is currently below 5 percent. Locking in on this number can lead to all sorts of conclusions

(95 percent plus employment is pretty terrific…Anyone not working must be lazy, and so on).

However, Gallup produces an enlightening statistic called the Gallup Good Jobs Index. It measures the percentage of the adult population that works over thirty hours a week for a regular paycheck, and the figure recently stood at 45 percent. So while the official jobs report suggests that unemployment is less than 5 percent, the Gallup survey tells us that 55 percent of adults don't have good jobs. And though these aren't exactly comparable datasets, they do help us appreciate the pitfalls of the illusion of knowledge.

Thoughts

There is always more to learn on any given topic. Strive to avoid rigidity in your thinking, and maintain an open mind.

CHAPTER 5

Always Choose the Right Thing

Walgreens was considering a partnership with Theranos Inc. when founder Elizabeth Holmes arrived at Johns Hopkins University. She brought with her a machine she said could test tiny samples of blood for dozens of conditions and thick binders of data to show its accuracy.

A Hopkins scientist told her that his researchers needed to put the device in their Baltimore laboratory to verify the technology on Walgreens' behalf, and Ms. Holmes agreed to provide one, say people familiar with the meeting.

It never happened. Walgreens wound up making a deal that included plans to put Theranos blood-testing centers in thousands of its drugstores across the

> United States, despite never fully validating the startup's technology or thoroughly evaluating its capabilities, according to people familiar with the matter. The relationship is now in tatters, making Walgreens an extreme case study of what can go wrong when an established company that craves growth decides to gamble on an exciting and unproven startup.
>
> —*Wall Street Journal*

⅄ ⅄ ⅄

Yes, Theranos' plunge in valuation of more than 90 percent is bad (from $9 billion to $800 million, according to *Forbes*). The hooey blood tests, possible federal sanctions, and criminal probes are worse. But there's also a lesson to be learned from the action, or inaction, exhibited by Walgreens. In the face of many questions and without performing the agreed-upon testing, Walgreens' leadership pushed forward reportedly because they were concerned that Theranos would partner with another drugstore chain if pressed too hard. A desperate desire for growth supplanted a thoughtful diligence process, and the fallout, to all parties, was staggering.

Leaders of an advisory practice can fall victim to the same thinking. Whether it's tunnel vision that overemphasizes growth, an outsized craving for profits, or some other obsession, you see how judgment can become clouded and how a firm can suffer catastrophic losses.

Managing and growing your practice are especially challenging. You're perpetually required to make decisions on a broad and rather random array of subjects (including investment offerings, personnel, trade errors, marketing strategies, and more). The fact is that even when you do your homework and engage in a thoughtful process, some of your decisions will prove to be wrong. Unfortunately, you won't always make the right decision, but you can always choose to do the right thing.

Thoughts

We sometimes describe our approach as "long-term greedy," and while on the surface this may come across as selfish, it's actually a great way to think about your practice. Having long-term greed means you want to build an enduring practice, which can only be achieved by making decisions that benefit your clients and your colleagues.

CHAPTER 6

Be Humble

Talent is God given. Be humble.
Fame is man-given. Be grateful.
Conceit is self-given. Be careful.
—John Wooden, coached UCLA basketball and won ten NCAA National Championships

▲ ▲ ▲

The egotistical boss. The rich guy who perpetually gloats. The superstar athlete who humiliates his opponent after a big play. The lack of humility is all around us, as are examples of when it comes back to bite someone.

Besides one's innate talents, there are many factors that contribute to success (think coaches, colleagues, timing, good fortune, and so forth). We easily fall into the trap of assuming we're solely responsible for our success, but this is dangerous for a variety of reasons:

1. A lack of humility creates resentment in others, making it difficult for them to be supportive when you need their help—and you will need help at some point.
2. As presented in chapter 3, being smart and hard-working doesn't provide a competitive advantage—such qualities are merely entry stakes. Maintaining a healthy organization is one of the few remaining competitive advantages. What's more, it's virtually impossible for collaboration, high levels of trust, and a lack of politics to exist when conceit and narcissism are present.

Thoughts

Humility is the only true wisdom
by which we prepare our minds for
all the possible changes of life.
—George Arliss

CHAPTER 7

Thoughtful Nepotism

Nep·o·tism: The practice among those with power or influence of *favoring* relatives or friends, especially by giving them jobs.

⅄ ⅄ ⅄

I find that some people are strongly opposed to nepotism in the workplace, while others routinely practice it (though it seems as if these folks often go ahead and hire family without giving it much thought). I prefer a middle ground that I'll refer to as "thoughtful nepotism."

If I take any offense to the definition of nepotism at the outset of this chapter, it's directed toward the word *favoring* in the context of hiring family or friends. I can tell you that some of our very best hires—including several who performed well and earned meaningful promotions—were relatives or friends of mine or others at our firm. So here are a few guidelines to help you navigate a slope that can become slippery.

The Good

- You know more about family and friends (and they know more about you), which typically produces a better understanding of potential fit.
- Hopefully, substantial trust and respect exist between you and any family or friend being considered for potential hire.
- The right relative or friend ideally has a better appreciation of you outside the workplace, which can add a positive dynamic.

The Bad

- Hiring relatives or friends who aren't *exceptionally* qualified for a role not only harms your enterprise but also ultimately causes frustration because it's unfair to them.
- Even qualified hires can evoke whispers of favoritism among the troops, and such gossip can be harmful to morale.
- Like any hire, sometimes things don't work out, and you're forced to let someone go. However, firing someone can be more challenging when that someone is a family member or friend.

Action Items

1. Have extremely candid discussions before an offer is made, and be certain to address the upside, the

downside, and what the plan would be if things don't work out.

2. Have the candidate articulate (in writing) his or her understanding of the role, the benefits, the potential pitfalls, and what the game plan would be if things don't work out.
3. Have your relative or friend report to someone other than you.
4. A relative or friend must be held to the highest standard that exists for everyone else—perhaps even a higher standard. If family members are not held accountable, even the most talented among them will be viewed as being favored, which damages team morale.
5. Never hire your child right out of school. My two sons recently graduated college (one with an economics degree and the other with a finance degree), and the subject of them working for me has never been broached. Thankfully, they're both gainfully employed, and candidly I'm not sure whether they'd ever have interest in working at our firm. Nevertheless, I feel strongly that it's better for them and for the company that they establish their own paths.

CHAPTER 8

Think. Care. Act.

> The difference between what makes an individual or a firm exceptional rather than merely good can be quite small. Think of Major League Baseball, where the difference between having a nice career and making it into the Hall of Fame can be the result of getting just one more hit per week. Or consider golf where the world's top-ranked players easily earn ten-times that of what good players, who average just one or two more strokes per round, earn.

⅄ ⅄ ⅄

Being smart and working hard are no longer competitive advantages—both are mere entry stakes in today's business world. What's more, entry stakes don't account for exceptional organizations or people. So what explains the difference? As previously addressed, fostering a healthy organization generates unique advantages across the enterprise. And I firmly believe that the abilities to *think*, *care*, and *act* are what separate exceptional professionals.

Plenty of great thinkers lead a variety of advisory practices, but do they care enough to habitually act on their good thoughts? There are so many unfortunate instances where valuable ideas fade before benefiting anyone. When you meet with a prospect or client and hear a colleague say something that could have been expressed better, do you note the occurrence and later coach him or her? If you experience a process at your firm that strikes you as inefficient, do you take the time to follow up and initiate improvement?

We all have good and even outstanding thoughts that could help clients, improve processes, educate colleagues, and so on—but thoughts aren't enough. If we seek to lead an exceptional firm, we need to care enough to act on our thoughts.

Action Items

When great ideas find you, schedule follow-ups to chase down the concepts. For example, during a recent and rainy Saturday morning, I was reading a golf magazine. I came upon a cartoon that prompted an idea for a column I write for one of our firm's newsletters. At that moment, I didn't have time to write the article, but I could not let this idea slip away. I grabbed my phone and scheduled an appointment with myself to write the article early the following week.

CHAPTER 9

Succession

> In the next ten years, nearly 15,000 advisors will retire each year. Yet more than 70 percent of advisors don't currently have a succession plan.
>
> —*Financial Advisor Magazine*

⅄ ⅄ ⅄

The vastness and potential complexity of succession planning may tempt you to look the other way. Don't. Because a thorough evaluation of options is beyond the scope of this book, let me instead share several powerful points I picked up in a presentation by Geoffrey Canada. Geoff is former president of the Harlem Children's Zone, in addition to being an author and social activist.

1. The organization must be better when you leave it.
2. If you love your organization, you will plan and then leave on its way up.

3. You/we are just a "piece" on the path to success:
   - If you're celebrated, you're fortunate.
   - Think of the folks who, for example, fought their whole lives against slavery and died before it ended. They still fought and advanced the effort, and that's what we need to do with our organizations.

Resource

The following, courtesy of Commonwealth Financial, nicely presents some of the more common succession strategies.

A range of options is available, depending on your preferences for the timing and level of involvement in the transition:

- **Sell and exit.** A common plan is to value your practice, sell it to another advisor, and retire. Occasionally, some retiring advisors will stay appointed and help introduce clients to the new advisor.
- **Merge and stay.** You can sell your practice—thus unburdening yourself of the costs and efforts associated with being a business owner—but stay on with the buying advisor, either to split business or as an employee.
- **Internal transition.** This option has attracted a lot of interest lately, because of books like *Succession Planning for Financial Advisors*, by David Grau Sr. Grau contends that 99 percent of practices will end with the practicing advisor's retirement or demise, unless an effort is made to develop an entity that outlives any individual advisor, much like the structure

of a law firm. This option requires a great deal of planning and dedication to transform the practice into a business, but the reward is a lasting legacy.

- **Partial sale.** If you love what you do, you may elect to keep your top clients and sell the majority of your client groups. This may be accomplished with or without the benefit of a merger. Some advisors do this in lieu of retirement, favoring instead this lifestyle practice.
- **Death or disability.** If you're in the "I'm never going to retire" crowd, consider putting together a plan that would transfer the business only in the event of death or permanent disability.

PART II

Practice Management

CHAPTER 10

Create an Organizational Chart of the Future

⅄ ⅄ ⅄

Many advisors run relatively small practices and have great aspirations for growth. One of the best things we did many years ago was create an organizational chart of what our future firm would look like; doing so helped to foster and process good growth.

At the outset, Bill Schneider, a few colleagues, and I performed pretty much every task in our firm. We didn't have marketing, research, or IT departments. No CFO. No head of analytics. No broad group of partners. Our firm was the typical small shop with big dreams.

Gerber Consulting prompted the idea of creating a futuristic organizational chart. They essentially had us identify all the duties in the firm and who was responsible for them. As you can imagine, a limited number of names ended up populating the entire chart (for example, I was CEO, Director of Manager Search, and an Institutional Consultant). The beauty of this approach was that as the firm grew, we would come to the realization that a given role had advanced beyond part-time status and required a "full body."

Resource

In addition to Org Chart templates built into Microsoft Office, many others can be found online:

www.e-myth.com
www.orgweaver.com
www.organimi.com

CHAPTER 11

Sell Every Day

Sell every day or the "factory" closes.

⅄ ⅄ ⅄

The principle of selling every day is something I adopted many years ago, and it's incredibly important. In leading your advisory practice, countless issues demand your time, and I'll bet that when you're not careful, it's easy to go home at night in a bit of a fog, wondering exactly what you accomplished that day.

I want to be clear: serving clients is crucial, as are many other duties, including enhancing investment strategy, practice management, hiring, mentoring, and so on. They're all crucial and they always will be. But what tends to get squeezed out of a busy day? That's right, selling! And if we don't have clients and revenues, none of the other stuff really matters, does it?

So, regardless of how busy we get, it's extremely beneficial to undertake at least one act of selling each business day. And there are so many ways to sell—for example, contacting a prospect in traditional fashion, though I also count acts like lunch with a center of influence (COI), and of course making a finals pitch to a prospective client. The key is to initiate at least one legitimate sales activity each day.

Now in the interest of full disclosure, I'll acknowledge that over the past ten years or so, I've been giving myself permission to *not* do any selling on Mondays, which have largely evolved into an administration day for me with a series of standing meetings. I find it useful to block out a specific day for such things, and doing so actually helps me be more productive the rest of the week.

Thoughts

> In any business organization, sales is the department that generates revenue. No matter how good your manufacturing operation is, how cutting edge your technology is, how tight your financial goals are, or how progressive and forward-thinking your management techniques are, you must still have a sales mechanism in place, or everything else is useless.
>
> —Chron.com

CHAPTER 12

Know When Good Is Good Enough

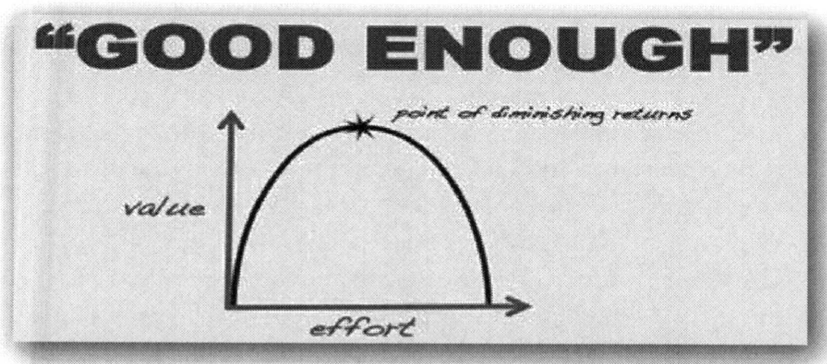

⅄ ⅄ ⅄

I hope this doesn't come across as boastful, but we've built an extraordinary firm. Of course I'm biased, but our sizable growth in assets under advisement and a 97 percent client-retention rate support my claim.[2]

A casual observer may assume we became extraordinary by being exceptional at *everything* we do. That assumption would be wrong. When mentoring younger professionals, I find that one of the more nuanced teachings is to know when *exceptional* output is required and when good is good enough. Our firm is filled with smart, hardworking people, so it's understandable why a young professional would, at times, turn a simple client request into an over-the-top task. But that doesn't make it right.

You and everyone on your team have limited capacity. Most of the time, client requests or questions can be swiftly and properly addressed. But sometimes these straightforward items become mounds of work instead, and the extra stress can be damaging in several ways. First, this unnecessarily erodes capacity. Next, it trains the client to expect extra output as status quo—even when the additional efforts are not useful. Finally, these young professionals may dupe themselves into thinking they're being productive, when in reality they're simply busy. Of course, all of this limits the growth of your practice in the long run.

Here are a few useful guidelines:

1. Talk with your team, and help them understand that properly navigating this topic can help them and the practice grow.

2. Teach your team that exceptional output is required in certain cases, so discuss the types of tasks, projects, and clients that should receive greater effort.
3. Inform your team that less than good is never acceptable.

Thoughts

> Good enough isn't necessarily a bad thing. In many areas of life, chasing perfection is a fool's errand, or at least a poor use of our time. We don't need to spend hours taste-testing every mustard on the gourmet shelf to find the absolute best; a good enough brand will suffice for our sandwich.
>
> —Marshall Goldsmith

CHAPTER 13

Never Mess with People's Pay

Why do people wake up in the morning, fix their coffee, and go to their jobs? Maybe they're passionate about their work; maybe they believe in what they're doing; maybe they're learning and developing before moving on to new opportunities. But likely, they have to pay their mortgage, put their kids through college, and save for retirement. While work is about so much more than pay, compensation is the foundation. Like Maslow's Hierarchy of Needs, we need sufficient pay before we can start to think about other "benefits"—like fulfillment and purpose.

—Mike Harden

⅄ ⅄ ⅄

I learned the following lesson many years ago, and it's very straightforward: never mess with your employees' pay. Advisory practice leaders can become inundated by a myriad of tasks, making it easy to rationalize why a paycheck was inaccurate, why a bonus wasn't paid on time, or even why the conversation you promised to have regarding pay keeps getting postponed. Don't overlook such things!

Pay can often become a very emotional topic for employees, and I can't blame them. Employees sacrifice or trade their personal and family time for compensation, so when you mess with their pay, they can feel disrespected, violated, and angry.

It's a given that firms should strive for 100 percent accuracy in processing routine payroll and bonuses, but sometimes frustration over compensation can be more nuanced. Perhaps your employee has taken on additional responsibilities and then develops an opinion that they're underpaid. Or perhaps the going rate in the marketplace has moved without you even being aware. Adding some structure that facilitates regular communication can help, and there are many ways to approach this. In addition to our open door policy, we conduct formal semi-annual reviews where associates are encouraged to raise any and all topics that are important to them.

Thoughts

Pay is the topic everyone cares about the most, whether they admit it or not. If you're not sure if that's true, imagine the decimal point on your next paycheck being moved one place to the left from where it normally is. How long would it take you to rearrange your priority list so that correcting the mistake is number one? Is there anything else in your work life you'd move to the top so quickly?

—Greg Richardson

CHAPTER 14

Sometimes You Need to Fire a Client

One day around my senior year in high school, I was assigned to caddie for a notoriously difficult club member. I'd seen him approaching and tried to hide behind the caddie shack, to no avail. I was stuck with him. On the sixth hole, he hit the ball into a water feature. He told me to go get it.

I'm not quite sure what got into me, but I responded by tossing his clubs into the water and telling him to go get those. Then I ran home. The caddie master later came to my house to speak with my parents. I was fired, of course—the end of my caddying career.

—Jack Welch, retired chairman of GE, on his first job as a caddie

⅄ ⅄ ⅄

We as advisors spend so much time and effort obtaining clients that our hard work makes firing clients seem counterintuitive. Letting a client go is an unfortunate occurrence that should transpire rarely—but sometimes it's the right thing to do.

Every so often, you find a mismatch between your offering and a client's desires; for example, you may utilize long-term investment strategies, but your client has more of a stock-picker mentality. Of course, good discovery in the prospecting phase and candid dialogue should identify the majority of these mismatches, but still expect to see them surface occasionally.

A much more damaging relationship is the client that simply can't be satisfied or—even worse—is highly unreasonable and aggressive toward you or your staff. This is especially tough for a service-centric organization, in which a "let's roll up our sleeves and help the client" mentality exits. However, these perpetually dissatisfied clients can zap the energy of your team and harm morale.

I'm not encouraging a quick trigger. On the contrary, consider the following if you find yourself becoming frustrated with a client:

1. Realize there are highs and lows in all relationships, and consider the possibility that these situations often change for the better.
2. Don't ignore problems indefinitely; consequences to your staff and organization can be substantial. Remember, we can't abdicate our leadership duties.

3. Sometimes having a simple and candid discussion with an excessively aggressive client works.
4. Before reaching the "firing stage," have a discussion along these lines:

> We value our client relationships, and we also have high conviction in our approach for long-term success. But if *you* are uncomfortable or anxious, we completely understand if *you* need to make a change.

If you're still facing issues after going through these steps, it's probably healthy for all parties to acknowledge the poor fit and to respectfully move on.

Thoughts

In some respects, I treat my work with clients like an act of service. We must place their interests first, and doing so extends beyond simply recommending sound investment strategies: sometimes we must labor to save them from themselves. Take a humble approach—that is, never let this concept turn into a pride thing. Be clinical, and if you must fire a client, do so humbly and respectfully.

CHAPTER 15

Compliance

> The good-heart, empty-head
> approach is a lousy defense.
> —Bill Schneider

⅄ ⅄ ⅄

An extensive exploration of compliance is far beyond the scope of this book, so I'll make a simple point: don't take compliance lightly and allow it to be the hurdle that trips you up!

1. Adopt meaningful and robust policies—and follow them!
2. Ensure that an attitude of good compliance permeates from the top of your organization.
3. You or a senior partner or colleague must take responsibility for internal oversight.

4. Hire outside firms, as necessary, to help develop policies, conduct mock audits, and so on.

Thoughts

> It is not enough, however, to have policies. You must also supervise your compliance program. Too often, the SEC runs across Chief Compliance Officers who are not competent and knowledgeable with the Investment Advisers Act and the rules thereunder.
>
> —National Compliance Regulatory Service

PART III

Hiring & Managing

CHAPTER 16

Bullseye Hiring Trap

We all know people are the most important resource in an advisory practice, and that's why many leaders expend great effort to foster a particular culture. Of course, growing the practice and adding people will impact culture, so here's a hiring pitfall to avoid: the *Bullseye Hiring Trap.* As taught to me years ago by Joe Deitch of Commonwealth Financial, the bullseye trap can wreak havoc when hiring is delegated to undisciplined or inexperienced managers. The concern is that even when a hiring supervisor is an "A Player" (however you define this), you run the risk of him or her stepping one ring outside the bullseye and adding a B player. Without proper training and direction, your practice could soon be far outside the bullseye in hiring, replete with C players or even D players.

⅄ ⅄ ⅄

Autonomy and trust are common elements of successful businesses; however, hiring is an area where I firmly believe intentionality and structure are required. Hiring may be your duty with the greatest risk: we all know how time consuming and mentally draining the wrong hire can be. You'll read more about creating a hiring system later, but suffice to say that I place such importance on hiring that no offer is extended to any candidate—at any level of our firm—before the supervisor personally meets with me and attests that he or she firmly believes the candidate truly satisfies our *Three Hiring Guideposts* criteria.

Thoughts

While it's absolutely true that a poor hire can waste thousands in hard-dollar recruiting, training, and other related costs, the toll on culture and morale may cause more damage than any monetary cost.

CHAPTER 17

How We Behave—Hiring Guideposts and More

As much as 80 percent of employee turnover is due to bad hiring decisions.
—*Harvard Business Review*

▲ ▲ ▲

While we strive to be thoughtful about all components related to hiring (think recruiting, interviewing, testing, checking references, onboarding, training, mentoring, and so on), there's one particular undertaking that's proven to have a profound effect, and this too was designed by Patrick Lencioni and his team. In developing our *Playbook* as Patrick describes it, the partners at our firm gathered to discuss and ultimately agree on an essential question: how do we behave? Sure, a variety of personalities and styles exist, which is good, but this exercise was about determining which fundamental characteristics are steadfast and mandatory for each professional at our firm. Of course, the *how we behave* is different for every organization.

Before sharing how to apply this to your own practice, let me first point out why it's so important. By identifying and then honoring your firm's indispensable behaviors, you'll make better hiring decisions, and you'll use this knowledge to make your practice better in many other ways. If these behaviors are the fabric of your firm, won't they also help with employee reviews, promotions, and even in evaluating a potential acquisition or merger?

Here's a great way to jump-start this process. Gather your partners (or senior managers) and ask them to think about your star employees. (You know the type—an employee who makes your job so much easier that you're glad they're part of the team.) Now, with these people in mind, write down the qualities that make you such a big fan. Are they dependable? Trustworthy? Creative? Kind? Maybe he or she is incredibly efficient or a real team player. Remember, attributes that one organization finds invaluable may not matter to another. The key is to engage in candid discussions with your partners or managers, in which you all ultimately agree on which characteristics distinguish your star performers.

I found this exercise to be relatively simple, and in a sensible amount of time, my partners and I settled on the following three required behaviors that all potential hires must have (and why the behaviors are important to us).

1. Can they **check their ego** at the door? Our highly collaborative environment relies on teamwork and communication.

2. Are they **accountable**? Autonomy provides professional stimulation and overall efficiency but fails without accountability.
3. Are they **thoughtfully driven**? We actually discussed this one for some time because the word *driven* can have negative connotations. Including the word *thoughtfully* communicates a desire to advance but not at the expense of others.

Of course, these qualities are considered in addition to pass or fail attributes, such as trust and effort. The items above became our main hiring guideposts, and as mentioned, they're used not only in every hiring decision but also in routine reviews and promotion considerations. Finally, these behaviors can't just be "good for the people who work for me." Partners and senior managers must live by them as well.

Resources

Harvard Business Review, "Make Your Values Mean Something", Patrick Lencioni

"8 Steps to Hiring Slow So You Don't Have to Fire Fast," www.LauraWage.com.

CHAPTER 18

Create a Hiring Strategy

A bad hire could cost up to five
times their annual salary.
—Society for Human
Resources Management

⅄ ⅄ ⅄

Hiring decisions certainly matter a lot, so it's puzzling that 95 percent of companies admit to recruiting the wrong people each year.[3] Missteps often begin even before a search commences because many firms lack a hiring strategy. One of the most important things you can do, as a leader, is to develop an intentional approach to hiring. Here is insight into our hiring protocol, which is intended to instill a consistent best-practices approach throughout our firm.

Always Be Recruiting: All advisory firms, even a small practice, need to think persistently about their next hire or replacement. Certainly partners should network and cultivate potential candidates, but hopefully everyone in your organization shows effort in the recruiting process. We pay bonuses to associates when their referrals are hired, as do other firms.

Phase I—Initial Steps

- Create Job Description *(hiring manager/HR)*
- Complete Hiring Form *(hiring manager)*
- Circulate the open position internally *(hiring manager)*
- Submit position to approved online hiring sites *(HR)*
- Retain recruiter if online resources are unsuccessful after two weeks *(hiring manager)*
- HR screens applications for hiring manager review *(HR)*

Phase II—Interview Process

- Screen qualified candidates by phone *(hiring manager)*
- Conduct initial office interview—maximum of three interviewers including hiring manager *(HR/hiring manager)*
- Assess promising candidates and document feedback *(hiring manger)*
- Administer The Predictive Index *(*PI—a tool we use to assess candidates' *fit* for a given role)
- E-mail candidates requesting second interview and completion of PI (*HR*)

- Schedule second interview—a minimum of two interviewers, including a partner (utilize interview form)
- Administer skill tests as appropriate
- Additional interviews as appropriate

Phase III—Hiring Process

- Draft offer letter (*hiring manager*)
- Complete Hiring Recommendation Form, after obtain managing director's approval *(hiring manager)*
- Check references *(hiring manager)*
- Send offer letter and attach benefits summary *(hiring manager/HR)*
- Submit background check *(HR)*
- Contact HR/IT for office and technology accommodations *(hiring manager)*
- Create Position Contract (*hiring manager/HR*)
- Announce new hire shortly before start date *(HR)*

Of course, each role can be a bit unique, and the approach can be modified (slightly) when appropriate. However, every candidate must complete the PI—it can account for 25 percent of the hiring decision—and the supervisor must meet with me to attest conviction that the chosen candidate possesses our three required behaviors.

Resource

The Predictive Index, www.predictiveindex.com

CHAPTER 19

Onboarding, Training, and Mentoring

An organization never gets a second chance to make a first impression with its new hires.

⅄ ⅄ ⅄

My wife is a CPA. She still recalls, with disdain, her first day at a new job: the desk and phone were filthy, and old ketchup packs, among other things, were scattered about. Obviously, it makes sense to properly onboard a promising candidate after you've invested great time and effort in hiring him or her. And good integration extends well beyond a clean and properly equipped workspace. Here are some worthy practices for properly onboarding a new employee:

- Even before their first day, circulate an internal e-mail with their bio and the role they'll play.

- Create a comfortable and well-equipped workspace.
- Craft an agenda for their first few days.
- Have a partner or senior professional (someone other than an HR or office manager) greet them on day one to welcome and provide an office tour.
- Conduct an HR meeting to address benefits, logistics, and so on.
- Have several of their department colleagues take the new hire to lunch.
- At 3:00 p.m., place basket of cookies at their desk. Distribute e-mail to colleagues requesting they stop by and introduce themselves.
- Provide the training schedule.

Training

We like to present a training schedule that includes both short-term and intermediate-term objectives. Things such as meeting with specific colleagues and reading the firm's research fall in the short-term category. It's very important to encourage new hires to take advantage of their slow initial pace and develop a thirst for knowledge. To foster this, we've created quite a few training videos using Camtasia and WebEx (see resources at the end of this chapter). These videos enable new hires to use their downtime effectively. It's also important to inform new hires that "the switch" from having time to train and absorb knowledge to being at full capacity can flip pretty swiftly, so embrace the learning.

Mentoring

Formal mentoring is a newer initiative for us, and I'd say that, by design, it's more of a mentor "lite" program. We want to provide a buddy of sorts to new hires, so we decided to appoint mentors from a different department, further expanding the contacts for new hires. We do recommend routine check-ins by the mentor and also encourage a mix of formal and informal touches. For us, it's simply good that new hires have one additional resource beyond their colleagues and supervisors.

Resources

Camtasia is a screen recorder that captures your clicks and your voice; it's a valuable training medium and can be found at www.techsmith.com.

WebEx is another option for creating training presentations.

CHAPTER 20

Management Practices

> Hire people who are better than you are, then leave them to get on with it...Look for people who will aim for the remarkable, who will not settle for the routine.
>
> —David Ogilvy

⅄ ⅄ ⅄

This chapter presents varied topics and principles useful in managing an advisory practice.

Hire right. Everything is easier if you hire people with skills and attitudes that align with your organization. Invest the necessary time and effort on the front end.

Train them up! I've always felt that in hiring there are only two options that offer a fighting chance for success—you can pay up to get experienced professionals, or you can hire less experienced people and invest the required time and energy to train them. I prefer the latter approach, but sometimes we find it appropriate to bring in experienced hires. If you also like to "grow your own," remember that to pursue this approach without a commitment to training is a long shot at best.

Pay matters. As noted in chapter 13, compensation is important to people, and good leaders understand that.

But pay isn't the only thing. Numerous studies show that while pay matters, it's certainly not the only thing that's important to employees. Respect, professional stimulation, opportunities for growth, an enjoyable environment, and more all contribute to employees' overall satisfaction.

Have empathy. Great leaders have a true understanding and appreciation for the challenges their teams face.

Have fun. All of us probably work a lot more than we play which makes it great when you can bring some fun into the workplace. Get creative with it! We occasionally have sundae bars at firm-wide meetings or close the office early for a "blow off some steam" afternoon, replete with food, manicures, massages, and shoe shines. Our team also enjoys participating in charity off-sites where our whole firm will pack food for shelters or some similar activity.

Lunch and learn. Professionals love to learn, and they love to eat. We'll regularly buy lunch and invite colleagues to attend informative presentations.

Wellness sessions. We strive to conduct three wellness workshops each year, and they're typically a big hit with colleagues. We've had "brain training," a fitness expert demonstrating how to fit workouts in while traveling, a nutritionist, and so on.

Be positive. I've never met anyone who is passionate about following a negative person.

Hold people accountable. Engage in open dialogue that produces known and realistic expectations—then hold your people to them. When deadlines and expectations aren't met, examine the cause (personal, structural, unavoidable?). Be respectful but firm. In our shop there are really only two acceptable approaches to deadlines. An assignment is either completed properly and on time, or a "hand gets raised" far enough in advance so we can collaborate on a solution.

Thoughts

> If you pick the right people and give them
> the opportunity to spread their wings—and
> put compensation as a carrier behind it—
> you almost don't have to manage them.
> —Jack Welch

CHAPTER 21

Inclusion and Diversity

I know of a large, highly regarded law firm that eventually recognized that every single partner in one of their offices was male and over six feet tall. That seemed a bit odd because the firm certainly didn't consider gender or height as qualifications for partnership. So what gives? As it turned out, that city had a basketball league for law firms, and a number of the partners loved to play. Naturally tall young male associates with basketball skills would be invited to join the team.

How do associates at law firms become partners? It's largely based on the clients they work with and the mentoring the associates receive. As you may appreciate, associates who played on the team got to know senior partners very well; leading to a high level of trust, and to frequently being selected to work on plum client assignments. Those who excelled were on a good path to partnership. So without ill intention—but perhaps with a simple desire to beat a rival law firm in a basketball game—certain associates were beneficiaries, and others clearly were not. Unintended consequences.

⅄ ⅄ ⅄

I've always believed that organizations run well as meritocracies, and this is especially applicable to advisory firms that pursue growth and a professionally stimulating environment. People should be promoted because of their abilities and talents rather than privileges or tenures. That said, I've come to understand that institutional biases exist in business, in our industry and, therefore, even in our firms. Simply put, not everyone has the same access to success.

Attempting to offset these institutional biases and unintended consequences goes beyond doing the right thing; it fosters a more inclusive workforce, which provides all kinds of benefits:

- Ideally, a firm's workforce demographics would be similar to the makeup of its clients. You can appreciate the importance of this if, for example, you're advising 401(k) plans, in which heads of HR are often female, or if you're working with private clients...

where women control more than half of the $14 trillion of America's personal wealth.[4]

- Even if your client base is not diverse, having a diverse group of professionals at your firm can be important to potential hires, especially millennials.
- Any successful inclusion and diversity initiative must start at the top.
- You also need support from junior and midlevel associates. Established white males might foster good goals and create a foundation, but younger professionals advance the movement.
- Don't make assumptions. For example, you really don't know if a woman with a young child would prefer not to travel unless you ask.

Thoughts

If you're willing to take a hard look at biases that are baked into the workforce, our industry, and your firm; listen and explore myths; and understand the hurdles to meritocracy that exist for some, then we're on to something.

PART IV

Marketing

CHAPTER 22

Marketing Matters

If a tree falls in a forest and no one is around to hear it, does it still make a sound?

If you develop an extraordinary investment strategy and no one adopts it, does it benefit anyone?

⅄ ⅄ ⅄

Some advisors are more quantitative by nature, and others are more qualitative, people oriented. Of course, both qualities are essential to success in this business. However, advisors who eschew marketing or perhaps view it as beneath them not only constrain the growth of their practice but also limit the number of potential clients that can benefit from their craft.

The simple truth is that marketing and sales matter. Now I fully appreciate that the type and style of business development you choose must be appropriate for your practice and fit your personality. But the bottom line is that we all need to market and sell.

As illustrated in upcoming chapters, there are many ways to generate business, and it's certainly not "one size fits all."

Thoughts

> Our job is to connect to people, to interact with them in a way that leaves them better than we found them, more able to get where they'd like to go.
>
> —Seth Godin

CHAPTER 23

Market to Existing Clients Too

In 2016 the auto industry will spend over $44 billion in advertising.[5] It's estimated that some luxury brands like Mercedes, direct nearly half their advertising budget toward existing customers.

⅄ ⅄ ⅄

Advisors often focus their marketing efforts on obtaining new clients, and that's certainly a worthy pursuit. However, it's a mistake to assume that your existing clients are all set and completely sold on your offering. It's important to continually market to them as well.

Of course, this type of promotion will differ from that of a prospective client. You're not introducing yourself, but you should provide meaningful updates and highlight the value you add. Think of Volvo regularly citing research that speaks to the safety of their cars. This communication reminds existing customers why they originally chose Volvo and, ultimately, that they should choose Volvo for future purchases.

Other advisors are constantly pursuing your clients, so marketing to existing clients is akin to playing good defense. Mention your new hires, professional promotions, technology updates, new articles, and speaking events. *Market* to your existing clients to reinforce their decision to work with you.

Thoughts

There are a variety of ways to market to your existing clients:

- Announce new hires and promotions.
- Distribute newsletters.
- Host webinars.
- Conduct seminars and workshops.
- Add firm highlights and achievements to your standard quarterly reports.
- Host social gatherings where clients can interact with one another.

CHAPTER 24

Institutionalize Your Marketing

For our firm's first dozen years or so, we were well intentioned about marketing. We'd loosely plan to write a certain number of newsletters, speak at various engagements, and so on. Of course, life and business would get in the way, and marketing routinely got bumped to the "back seat." The financial crisis of 2008 is what ultimately helped us institutionalize our marketing efforts, and our firm has experienced exponential growth ever since.

⅄ ⅄ ⅄

It's important to appreciate that marketing efforts, both to prospects and existing clients, are essential to the success of your practice. It's also human nature to do what we used to do—allow marketing initiatives to falter—but that can be damaging. Here are several considerations for your marketing.

1. If you buy into the premise that growth is essential (if for nothing more than to attract and retain quality professionals), then you must adopt a strategy to obtain new clients. And that strategy is marketing, of course.
2. You must always replace clients, whether doing so is the result of a corporate merger, death, or simply a poor fit. Accept that you'll forever need to replace clients in this business.
3. Treat your marketing commitments (for example, your production of newsletters or "touch points" with centers of influence) as seriously as you treat your other commitments.
4. Create a multifaceted blueprint for marketing (see chapter 26).
5. Add a body…or two! You can't do it all. If you try to, marketing will almost certainly be the initiative that gets ignored. Many practice leaders are concerned with the potential costs associated with designated marketing hires; however, the right marketing professionals will contribute to your bottom line in a meaningful way.

Thoughts

> There are no magic wands, no hidden tricks, and no secret handshakes that can bring you immediate success, but with time, energy, and determination, you can get there.
>
> —Darren Rowse, founder of PROBLOGGER

CHAPTER 25

Focus on What's Important to Them!

> When you start with what's at stake for the buyer, you earn the right to their attention.
>
> —Jake Sorofman

⅄ ⅄ ⅄

Most of us are passionate about what we do; while that's a good thing, it can make us blind to the needs of our prospects or even our centers of influence who introduce us to prospects. Here's an insightful story that one of my talented colleagues recently shared with me. It illustrates the importance of creating a relationship before trying to sell anything.

> I've come to realize that in the past, I have been too focused on trying to sell a prospect or a COI on why we're the best. More recently, I shifted my approach to focus on developing a personal relationship first,

then waiting for natural opportunities to discuss business. As an example, I had lunch recently with a COI who spent the whole time talking about his kids' sports and things I should consider for my kids, as they are nearing the age where they can begin to participate in organized sports. In the past, I would have tried to shift the conversation back to business, but instead I just let it flow. As a result, I learned a lot more about the COI than I would have otherwise. We have more to talk about in the future, and I have numerous touch points that I wouldn't have otherwise had; this will foster good conversations down the road.

Thoughts

Steve Satkamp, one of my bosses at Kidder Peabody, shared this sage advice and it's as important today as it was twenty-five years ago: "People do business with people they like, they trust, and they believe can help them…in that order!"

CHAPTER 26

Adopt a Multifaceted Approach

> Instead of one-way interruption...marketing is about delivering useful content at just the precise moment that a buyer needs it.
>
> —David Meerman Scott, *The New Rules of Marketing and PR*

⅄ ⅄ ⅄

To be certain, any marketing plan must begin with a true understanding of the clients you serve or intend to serve. Our clients include retirement plans, nonprofits, and wealthy families, in addition to the outsourced chief investment officer (OCIO) services provided to a select number of financial institutions. Of course we further define our target market by desired size, type, and even moxie (we seek clients who are smart, busy, and willing to pay for expertise).

Once you clearly identify your target market, it's important to implement a multifaceted marketing strategy. Various mediums resonate with people differently, so we choose to deliver a consistent message to a target audience, using a broad-based approach. I can't emphasize enough that the message doesn't change—only the deliverable. Here are some examples:

- **White Papers.** These typically resonate with our more technical clients.
- **Newsletters.** We have five unique newsletters (by client type) that give us the opportunity to show the firm's personality in addition to our expertise.
- **Quarterly Considerations.** We provide routine market and economic updates, which clients expect.
- **Knowledge College.** Produced quarterly, these deliver a brief but meaningful examination of an important subject.
- **Workshops.** These are among our most successful initiatives. It's terrific when clients, prospects, and COIs are all interacting on topics important to them.
- **Annual Investor Conference.** Think of this as a workshop on steroids, and we always enjoy a capacity crowd.
- **Website.** Meaningful content and calls to action are vital.
- **Conference Calls and Webinars.** These communications efficiently share knowledge on timely, ad hoc topics.
- **Videos.** They've become incredibly popular with clients, prospects, and our financial institutions. We keep them short, relevant, and timely. (Our

three-minute Brexit video was distributed before 10:00 a.m. on the morning of the decision.)

As shown, there are a variety of ways to share knowledge with your targeted audience, and each method is important to someone! People don't want to be "sold to." You greatly increase the odds of having your hat in the ring if you regularly deliver valuable content. A prospect will naturally consider you when they become ready to buy.

Action Items

You may be growing tired of me repeatedly emphasizing the importance of marketing. Here are a few suggestions that even non-marketers can take to heart.

1. **Put a capable professional in charge of your marketing efforts.** Don't use someone who will try and do it "on the fly" while juggling clients and other duties. This is a bona fide position charged with promoting your value to prospects, clients, and centers of influence.
2. **Create a marketing calendar.** Identify the desired frequency of newsletters, workshops, white papers, and so on; schedule production and release dates, and have your marketing professional "ride herd."
3. **Make marketing a measurable duty for everyone, including your advisors.** A great deal can be offloaded to your marketing professional, but that person can't do it all. He or she will need others to contribute

content, speak at conferences, meet with COIs, and more. We're thoughtful about not overly burdening our advisors, but marketing must be a team effort. We establish realistic objectives and then assess progress in our semi-annual employee reviews.

CHAPTER 27

Pricing Matters

Advisors
36%
Are being asked for more transparency1
43%
Say they need to provide more services in order to maintain current pricing1

Fidelity Advisor Community Pricing Research, 2015

⅄ ⅄ ⅄

As the graphic above illustrates, transparency in pricing is a growing trend, as is the need to provide greater value. The survey results bring to mind the old adage: *price* is only an issue in the absence of *value*. Here are several other important considerations relating to pricing.

1. **Transparency is absolutely growing in importance.** Embrace it and discuss pricing with your prospects and clients.
2. ***Cost* is less offensive.** Studies show that terms like *fee* and *charge* are offensive to consumers. On the other hand, people know there are costs associated with thoughtful purchases. Your marketing materials should favor the term *cost*.
3. **Continually improve your offering**. Look no further than the computer you currently use to appreciate how important it is to continually advance your value proposition. An advisor should look at the cost and capabilities of computers today compared with those from a decade ago and then ask if his or her advisory services are advancing in similar fashion.
4. **Run a tight ship.** With robo-advisors and all types of additional competition, it's important to be thoughtful about expenditures.

Thoughts

Pursue the right type of client. The amount of work it takes to serve both high-margin and low-margin clients can be similar—so why not target clients that fit well with your practice and generate appropriate margins?

PART V

Investing

Author's Note: Given the many viable investment strategies, this section purposefully presents principles and concepts that apply universally.

Strategies presented do not in any way represent investment recommendations. Any reference to investment performance is generic in nature. Past performance does not guarantee future results. Information is obtained from a variety of sources believed though not guaranteed to be accurate.

CHAPTER 28

The Danger of Extrapolation

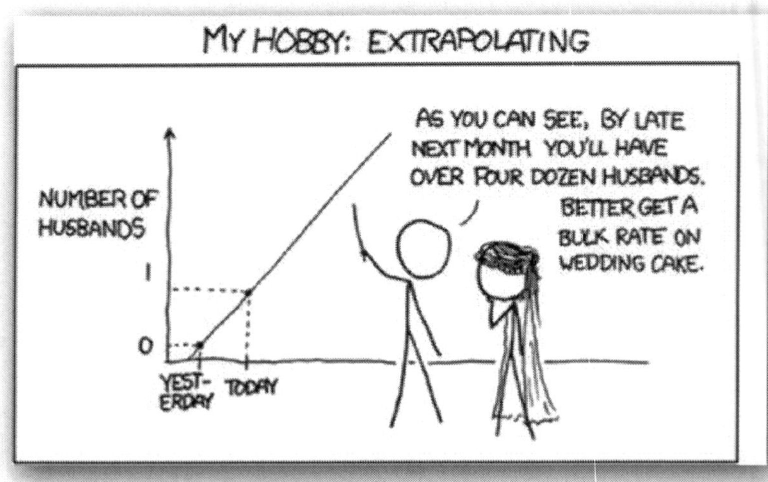

⅄ ⅄ ⅄

As humans, we often disproportionately rely on recent occurrences to shape our thoughts concerning future events. But when investors, or even worse clients, use short-term results to forecast, it can be damming to a well-conceived investment strategy.

I get it. It's so tempting for clients to draw conclusions from recent performance. For example, take a look at large-cap US stocks as represented by the S&P 500. Following the financial crisis, they were "the place to be," and through June 2015, the index averaged more than 17 percent annually over the preceding five years. Clients were left wondering why they even owned a diversified portfolio—shouldn't they exclusively invest in large-cap stocks?

Yet if you looked at returns in mid-2009, the S&P 500 averaged a *loss* of 2.2 percent over the prior five years. People back then were questioning why they'd ever want to own large-cap US stocks.

I often share a story about Elvis impersonators with clients to drive home the hazards of extrapolation. You may not be aware that the first known Elvis impersonator appeared on the scene way back in 1956. There were reportedly one hundred impersonators in the '60s and 170 at the time of Elvis' death in 1977. Then things really started to roll, and the number expanded to more than thirty-five thousand in the nineties. If this rate of growth had persisted, then by sometime around the year 2020, one-third of Americans would be walking around as Elvis impersonators! I like the Elvis example because it helps us appreciate how silly extrapolating recent trends can be.

Thoughts

Remind clients that investment extrapolation is like soup du jour. Whether it's large-cap stocks, real estate, or passive/active investing, there's always some hot trend that's tempting to extrapolate. Be warned though—extrapolation can wreak havoc on a portfolio.

CHAPTER 29

Don't Piss in the Wind

I recall having a conversation with the founder of a good-sized and successful advisory practice in the Northeast. They had just one CFA charterholder on staff, and the founder was contemplating whether to engage our firm as their "research engine" or to hire a second charterholder. The mismatch between the size of their practice and its research effort was almost comical—adding one more individual wasn't going to move the needle.

⅄ ⅄ ⅄

When you look at our *entire* firm, roughly 40 percent of us have obtained or are pursuing the CFA designation, and that's in addition to all the CIMAs, CFPs, MBAs, CAIAs, and CPAs. I'm the last person to discourage anyone from building a robust research effort, though I firmly believe it's essential to either make a legitimate commitment or to outsource your research. Here are several considerations:

1. What are you passionate about? A love of analysis and investments may suggest building an internal effort, while those who cherish client interaction or business development should consider outsourcing.
2. Can your internal effort compete? I personally work with institutional clients, and for years it's been common to respond to their RFPs for new business. Now, families and even individual investors are issuing questionnaires. Can your research effort stand up to the scrutiny?
3. Do you have access to talent? Are you geographically located in a place that talented professionals find desirable?
4. What about cost? It shouldn't be the driving factor, but you need to know the delta between outsourcing and building a genuine internal effort.
5. If you choose to staff your own research department, can the effort serve your clients well, in a way in which you would be proud?

Thoughts

If you decide to outsource research, know that success will absolutely depend on the fit between your practice and the firm you hire. Do your investment philosophies align? (They should, at least on vital matters.) Is the firm willing to help you grow? Can it provide solutions that are unique to your practice and your clients' needs?

CHAPTER 30

Don't Give Them Brown Shoes!

"If he wants brown shoes, sell him brown shoes!" This old saying refers to selling a customer what he or she wants...even if it's not right. Have you ever taken so much heat from a client regarding a recommendation or strategy that it would be easier to simply cave in and let them make a poor decision? Don't!

⅄ ⅄ ⅄

I remember meeting with a client back in January 2009—a time, as you may recall, when stocks were free falling, and no one knew when we'd hit bottom. The client was a large religious institution; in fact, the investment committee consisted of eleven smart, well-intentioned nuns.

Well, this meeting should have lasted about ninety minutes, but instead ran more than four hours! Given all the uncertainty, the nuns were dead set on shifting the portfolio from approximately 70 percent growth (equities and alternatives) and 30 percent bonds to just the opposite, with 70 percent in fixed income. Now, it was not our money, nor was it our role to tell the client to be conservative or risky. However, it is our role to profoundly comprehend what this client was attempting to accomplish—in this circumstance, primarily to advance their missions around the world. They wanted to develop an investment strategy that would give them a fighting chance of achieving their goals.

I understood their mission and also understood their concern over the portfolio—it was declining substantially in value. This meeting went on and on because I insisted that they should identify what they would cut from their budget if they intended to shift to an allocation with a much lower long-term expected return. Again, it was their money, but if their investments earned less than half of the original target, they would be unable to advance the missions for which we budgeted.

After hours of urging them to think through this potentially dangerously reactive decision, I finally said, "I'd rather you get this decision right and fire us because you think I'm pushy rather than not get it right." They ultimately grasped and appreciated my input and decided to stick with both their mission and the allocation that was crafted to support it. Of course, the market bottomed in March of that year, just a couple months after our marathon meeting, and their decision to avoid being dangerously reactive led to great gains, helping them achieve their goals in support of their mission.

Thoughts

The nuns realized excellent gains. Some may mistake what happened for smart timing or some exceptional market call on our part—but their success wasn't that at all. It was simple, though not easy, and incorporated the following:

1. Embrace a discovery process that identifies the client's overarching objectives and mission.
2. Develop a financial strategy and a well-constructed portfolio that provide a fighting chance of success.
3. During periods of stress, invest time and energy to help clients reconcile the mission they articulated with the actions they're considering.

CHAPTER 31

Client Meetings

I am sufficiently proud of my
knowing something to be modest
about my not knowing all.
—Vladimir Nabokov, *Lolita*

⅄ ⅄ ⅄

Terrific performance for the quarter! It's a great thing, and it's also a slippery slope. Advisors can be tempted, especially with a challenging client, to overemphasize good performance at a quarterly meeting. Don't.

It's important to avoid taking too much credit for results in a good quarter. Instead, I like to compliment the client on the prudent plan *they* adopted, and I also use the opportunity to discuss the ups and downs of any strategy, as well as the benefits of long-term, strategic thinking.

Thought

Intelligence could be more
brilliant within modesty.
—Toby Beta, *Master of Stupidity*

CHAPTER 32

Coach Your Clients on Downside Risk

We've long felt that the only value of stock forecasters is to make fortune tellers look good. Even now, Charlie and I continue to believe that short-term market forecasts are poison and should be kept locked up in a safe place, away from children and also from grown-ups who behave in the market like children.
—WARREN BUFFET

⅄ ⅄ ⅄

Since the Dow Jones Industrial Average was introduced in 1896, it's increased two out of every three years on average. And with annualized returns of around 8 percent,[6] investors can and have amassed incredible sums over the long haul. But there's a dark side to realizing gains in most years. It means that, on average, stocks decline every third year.

I find it's useful to remind clients of downside risks, not only at the outset of a relationship but also and especially when markets perform well. Be clear that you're not forecasting a long-term bear market; instead, use this opportunity (when stocks are on a roll) to provide a few commonsense reminders:

1. **Expect downturns.** Remind clients, in advance, that stocks periodically fall; doing so can help them withstand the emotional roller-coaster ride that accompanies investing.
   - Despite annualized returns in the high single digits (contingent on the time frame, so let's call it 8 to 10 percent), the S&P 500 averages intra year *declines* of over 14 percent![7]
   - Even with average intra year drops of over 14 percent, the S&P 500 realized positive returns in twenty-seven of thirty-five years.[8]
2. **Know your downside.** Do clients know how poorly their portfolio may perform in a downturn? Show them, given their current allocation, the historical worst month, year, and peak-to-trough declines. Better to have this knowledge at the outset, or when stocks are rallying, to encourage informed decisions.
3. **Adjust if necessary.** Discussing how much a portfolio may decline is important and logically leads to asking a client whether they believe they can tolerate such losses, even if the losses are likely temporary.

- It's useful to consider potential losses in dollar terms rather than percentages—clients don't spend percentages.
- If the potential loss associated with a current allocation is not tolerable and the client elects to shift to a lower-risk portfolio (with lower expected returns), this move must be accompanied by one of two options: either increase *inflows* or cut *outflows*.

It's always good to discuss the appropriateness of the current investment strategy and remind the client that while stocks, on average, increase two out of every three years, simple math tells us that stocks will tumble from time to time.

Resource

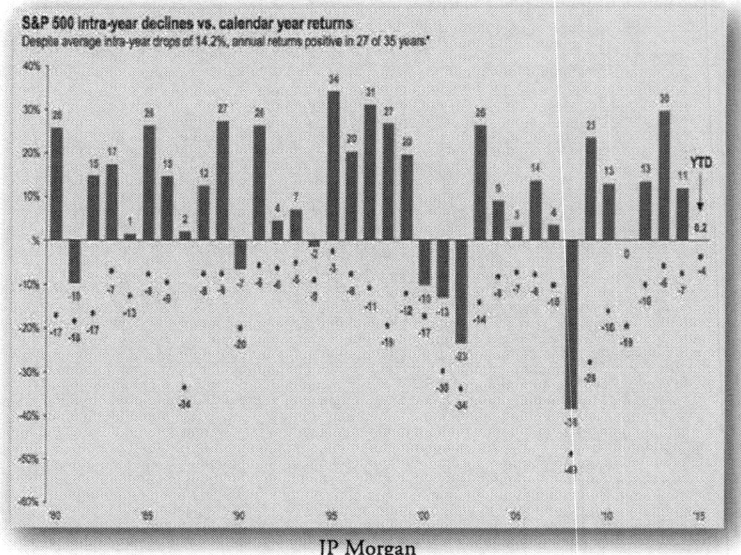

JP Morgan

CHAPTER 33

Push Back...Sometimes

> And if any place will not welcome
> you or listen to you, leave that place
> and shake the dust off your feet
> as a testimony against them.
> —Jesus, Mark 6:11

⅄ ⅄ ⅄

Sometimes you do everything correctly for a client, but the relationship is still strained. I'll share a story to illustrate. I introduced a high net-worth client to one of my extremely capable partners in our private client practice. He and his team did an exceptional job of onboarding. From thorough discovery that identified the client's needs, to candid discussions regarding risk, to seamless transition and implementation, this client received "gold star" treatment.

Unfortunately, timing was such that the client came to us just before the onset of a market pullback. Even though our team had outlined both the expected volatility and the need to adopt a long-term perspective, the new client panicked over a modest decline in his portfolio. His fear became extreme, requiring my partner to have lengthy discussions with the client nearly every evening following a down day in the market. My partner would remind the client of not only the return targets *he* had adopted but also the historical and forecasted downside that had been discussed. The client would acknowledge his trepidation was unreasonable and apologize for wasting everyone's time. However, if the market declined the following day, he'd be right back on the phone in a panic. The situation became stressful to both my partner and the entire team working with this client.

Here are a few ways to navigate stressful client situations (or perhaps prevent them):

1. **Properly pursue.** Sometimes you can tell, even in early stages, that a prospect simply is not a fit for your approach. This doesn't make them bad or evil…just a poor fit, and recognizing this early on can save a lot of heartache for all.
2. **Properly onboard.** This is the time to have extremely candid discussions regarding risk. Also, challenge clients on their return targets—that is, do they really need to shoot for as high a return as they initially communicate?
3. **Empathize.** A risk in talking to your team and placing any fault on clients, even if justified, is that the team's mind-set can evolve to "the client's always wrong." Of course this isn't so. Everyone must work

hard to appreciate client concerns, and respond to them appropriately.

4. **Dust off your sandals.** Occasionally, you'll need to have a "come to Jesus" discussion with a client. When necessary, I prefer the following sort of language because it not only reminds clients of the thoughtful strategies that have been adopted but also tosses the ball in their court to determine the next steps:

   > We're confident in our approach, and history shows that it's worked over the long term. You selected a prudent strategy, based on the needs you articulated. However, if this is causing too much stress or you can't sleep well at night, I understand if *you* need to make a change.

Thoughts

> Where they were received with joy, they should stay and teach. But where their message was rejected, they had no further responsibility. They were free to walk away with a clear conscience, knowing they had done all they could do.
>
> —Interpretation of Mark 6:11; www.gotquestions.org

CHAPTER 34

Investment Returns—Only Part of Your Value Add

The typical PGA touring professional's fairway accuracy is less than 60 percent, and nearly every pro hits fewer than 70 percent of fairways off the tee.[9] Likewise, no investment strategy works 100 percent of the time. Advisors must bring more than performance to the game.

⅄ ⅄ ⅄

Solid investment performance is essential, but relying solely on investment returns can be perilous to your practice—and to your clients' well-being. I'm extremely proud of our research professionals, and I hold their analytical skills up to any group in the business. Despite their intellect and talent, our investment strategies don't outperform 100 percent of the time...not even close.

We diligently monitor the results of our asset-allocation methodology, and find that our thoughtful and broad allocations tend to outpace narrowly diversified strategies, and typically with less risk. While that's good, no approach is superior in all environments—that is, there certainly are periods when we underperform.

Here are several suggestions to help you and your clients endure off-periods of performance.

1. **New clients.** Be thorough in your discovery and goal setting phase and take this opportunity to set expectations, to discuss market cycles, and so on.
2. **Have an extraordinary service model.** You've seen the many studies that demonstrate how poorly the typical investor performs. While average performance is not something to strive for, I believe most advisors would have more than enough business if they could simply couple average returns with extraordinary service.
3. **Build relationships.** Remember that people do business with people they like, they trust, and they believe can help—in that order! What are you left with during down periods if you focus exclusively on returns?
4. **Educate.** Sharing knowledge is another way to provide value to clients. Whether workshops, videos, webinars, or newsletters, regularly help your clients increase their understanding of topics that are *important to them.*

Expanding your focus beyond investment returns will greatly benefit your practice—but doing so will also benefit your clients. Adopting this strategy helps build equity with a client, which in turn helps them avoid dangerously reactive decisions when returns temporarily wane. That's good for you, as well as your clients' financial future.

Thoughts

Of course, good food is essential at a restaurant I choose to dine at, but for me the experience is about so much more than just the meal. The setting and service matter greatly. I also appreciate feeling welcome and respected. All these factors and more help create a positive experience and contribute to a restaurant becoming one of my favorites. Think of your investment advisory practice in the same manner.

PART VI

Life Balance

CHAPTER 35

Priorities—Set Them (or at Least Acknowledge Them)

> An alcoholic man, whose wife and children are desperately in need of him at that very moment, may be sitting in a bar with tears in his eyes, telling the bartender, "I really love my family."
>
> Love is as love does.
>
> —M. Scott Peck, *The Road Less Traveled*

⅄ ⅄ ⅄

I don't present this caption from Peck's insightful book as commentary on alcohol. Instead, it strikes me as a piercing illustration of how muddled our priorities may become—and how we're pretty good at fooling ourselves.

What are your priorities in life? Do you ever wonder how consistent your daily actions are with your stated priorities? One revealing method for assessing priorities is to examine both your calendar and your checkbook. It's pretty difficult to argue that where you spend the majority of your time and money isn't important to you. Those are your priorities, at least for now.

Action

If you're pleased with your priorities and how you're spending your time and money, that's great. But if you have the notion that you could or should have different, perhaps even better, priorities, there's work to do. I encourage you to invest time on your Life Plan (chapter 36). Life is short—let's avoid regrets.

CHAPTER 36

A Life Plan

Creating a plan for your business but not your life may very well lead to regret.

⅄ ⅄ ⅄

Some people are incredibly good planners. They develop business plans, social plans, and even extensive plans for their children. So doesn't it strike you as odd that many of these same individuals never develop a plan or mission for their own lives?

I'm probably an above-average (but by no means exceptional) planner. But I feel that I "nailed it" in one area, and that's in developing a mission or overarching plan for my life. At the risk of sounding immodest, I'll share my own life plan to help you understand how meaningful your plan can be in shaping many parts of your life. (There's some reservation in sharing my plan because life plans should not be competitions. They're deeply personal; they're driving forces in the way we think and act.)

If you're concerned, please know we're not going to venture too far down the touchy-feely path. Creating a life plan begins with brutally honest reflection on what is important to you. Obviously you must thoughtfully engage which requires time and a clear mind. Even though the seeds for your life plan likely exist already and you've probably spent some time thinking about it, crystalizing your plan requires intentionality and usually occurs over time.

Once again, the brutally honest component is extremely important—remember, it's your life. If your personal mission is to spend countless hours with your children, that's great. If it's to become the richest advisor you know, then go for it. The only way to develop an enduring plan, one that aligns all facets of your life, is to be honest about what's important to you.

I wish to be candid with my experience. After a good amount of personal reflection, and then, candidly, something I simply felt in my heart, I realized: I was put on this planet to help others. There are many ways in which my plan can manifest itself (for example, taking time to truly listen to a friend, volunteering, helping clients prosper, and making financial donations to worthy causes). While helping others became my mission, my main guidepost in my life, the supporting principles are equally important. Let me explain. If my goal truly is to help others, then I must possess the *ability* to help. This led to my developing an expanded mission incorporating this essential principle:

> Be mentally, physically, and financially fit so that I can help others.

Uniting my life plan with my underlying principle has been incredibly effective over the years. Take the "mentally fit" component. All of us would agree that it's very difficult to help someone else if we ourselves are not in a solid mental state. But when you link principles into your life plan, they take on elevated importance. At some point, I began to realize that overscheduling and operating at an unsustainable pace ran counter to being mentally fit, which in turn was in direct opposition to my mission. Likewise, being hyper busy and skipping workouts also became an attack on my life plan.

If you view things in this light, you will increase your awareness and begin to align day-to-day activities with your life plan. For example, it became easier for me to say no to a nice but unnecessary invitation to a business dinner or similar events. I also began to treat my workouts with the same level of importance as other appointments (again, it's challenging to help others if you're physically ill). And my being a good financial steward (of clients' portfolios and my own) became paramount to my ability to help others.

Developing a life plan has broad reach and will certainly translate to the management of your practice. Again, by continually recalling my main purpose, to help others, I'm expected and even emboldened to do the tough things at work. For example, I don't have the luxury of not dealing with a challenging employee. My main goal is to help others, so I must engage, constructively, with employees and attempt to arm them with the skills and resources they need to succeed at our firm. If my efforts are unsuccessful and if I ultimately realize that a certain employee fits poorly at our firm, I can't abdicate my duties (I'm not helping an employee when I prolong a mismatch, and I'm certainly not helping my other seventy colleagues that depend on our firm being successful.)

It's Your Plan, and It May Evolve

When developing your life plan, keep these two points in mind:

1. Your first thought may be to make your life plan an altruistic mission, but if that's not truly important to you, your plan will be unsustainable. Again, be exceedingly honest about what's vital to you.
2. It's likely that your plan, or at least your underlying principles, will evolve over time. For example, I've come to appreciate that while my mission may be to help others, I may need to modify an underlying principle, like physically fit, as circumstances warrant.

Action Items

Take some time to answer the following questions to prime the pump in developing your life plan.

1. What do I enjoy most?
2. What am I most grateful for?
3. What am I most committed to?
4. What am I most excited about?
5. Who do I love?
6. Who loves me?

CHAPTER 37

Unsustainable—Sometimes Change Is Required

At our firm, partners work with clients and also have some type of firm-level responsibilities. For example, one of my partners is an institutional consultant and also has partner responsibility over our Core Research team. Another partner oversees our institutional consulting effort, in addition to his client load. I work with clients and am managing director of the firm.

Back in 2008, just about the time the Great Recession (and the worst bear market in seventy years) was unfolding, my co-founder, Bill Schneider, was coincidentally transitioning his schedule to part time and toward retirement. We decided I'd assume Bill's partner responsibility for marketing. A proactive approach would be important in this market downturn, and I was up for the challenge. Besides, I've always enjoyed the creativity and science involved in good marketing strategies, and we had two terrific colleagues dedicated to that department.

This turned out to be an exciting and successful endeavor. With great effort by our marketing team and many others, we thoroughly enriched our approach to marketing. For the next few years, I maintained partner responsibility for marketing, in addition to my duties as managing director and, of course, my work with clients (in a rather challenging and demanding market environment).

Marketing was excelling, the firm was humming along, and clients were happy and being served well (we conduct periodic surveys). But my stress level was growing, and managing my schedule became nearly impossible. It was almost like a slowly boiling pot of water; I didn't appreciate or fully realize what had hit me, but the combination of additional partner duties on top of heightened sensitivity to client needs in challenging markets had created an unsustainable pace for me. Something had to change.

⅄ ⅄ ⅄

I don't know if it's because many entrepreneurs have an innate ability to develop solutions, or maybe it's a stubborn guy thing ("I can handle this!"), but strong traits that help us persevere can at times be detrimental. By definition, we can't continue at an unsustainable pace for long durations. But an unsustainable pace can almost creep up on you. I'm somewhat embarrassed that I had to have a light-bulb moment to realize that taking on marketing-related partner duties besides my full-time gig (clients and managing the firm) was simply too much. We decided to have a newer partner assume marketing responsibilities, and his background made him a perfect fit. Almost instantly, my schedule became manageable, and we simultaneously brought a fresh perspective to our marketing efforts.

At times, we all can feel overwhelmed by our workload, but here are a couple ways to manage:

1. **Determine if your overwhelmed state is temporary or originating from a structural problem.** Certain markets require more effort, and onboarding new clients can squeeze your calendar. These sorts of things generally fall into the temporary camp. But when you find you're "running hot" for extended periods and not able to catch up, pause and assess your situation. Did you (as I did with marketing) take on new duties and not delegate others? Or perhaps growth merits "adding a body" for something you used to do on a part-time basis. If you're overwhelmed for extended periods, come up for air, and evaluate what you can change structurally.
2. **Neither a crisis nor your involvement should be permanent.** I completely understand that issues will arise that demand your attention. You care about

your practice and are willing to jump in when duty calls. Though be careful about *staying* longer than necessary. It comes down to simple math: nothing is wrong with taking on new duties…as long as you offload others.

Thoughts

Just because you're good at something (or enjoy it) doesn't mean you should be doing it. The fact that I'm professionally stimulated by marketing probably contributed to the length of time it took me to realize I had taken on a meaningful endeavor without removing any other responsibilities. Be fair to yourself and assess things.

CHAPTER 38

He Who Angers You Conquers You

It happens quite often: you're driving down the road, minding your own business, when another car abruptly swerves into your lane. You slam your brakes, narrowly avoiding an accident, and proceed to yell some profanity at the other driver. In these close encounters, you're all at once startled, scared, and pissed off. Now, imagine the other driver being completely unaware of any wrongdoing. He or she simply continues on his or her merry way while you're left with a racing heart and mad as hell. In a sense, the oblivious driver angered and conquered you—or at least your attitude and mind-set.

⅄ ⅄ ⅄

This sort of experience can occur regularly in our professional and personal lives, and it's tough for many to handle. Some take pleasure in expressing anger and in unloading on the wrongdoer, but I find that's one of the least productive things we can do. Putting aside the benefits of treating others in humane fashion, I'm surprised at how many people allow their emotions to control them. Do professional golfers or neurosurgeons perform better when they're really angry? Of course not! And neither do we as advisors, employers, spouses, parents, or friends.

Now, I'm not suggesting you let people steamroll you or that you not hold others accountable for their actions; however, there are more productive ways to approach this:

1. Fully appreciating the visual of the oblivious guy going about his merry way while I'm left upset and angered helps me manage my emotion. I commit to not allow anger, or the other guy, to control me.
2. There are random experiences (like the person who cuts you off) in which we simply have to "box up" the emotion and let go, because it harms us more if we don't. However, there are other circumstances in which we should take action—but the right kind of action. In a business relationship, you might contractually address areas of particular concern that will cause you frustration or anger if they are not performed properly. This can be helpful in many settings, including overseeing employees and even raising children.

Thoughts

You shouldn't have to choose between maintaining your sanity and attaining the results you want. Let me provide an example. I volunteer for Year Up, a terrific nonprofit organization. In short, they help low-income young adults, empowering them to go from poverty to professionals in a single year. The results are staggering: a participant can advance from average annual earnings of $7,500 before they enter the program to $36,000 in just one year! As you may imagine, these young adults are required not only to learn a lot but also to be punctual, dress properly, and so on. Each student is allotted a certain number of points; additional points can be earned for things such as good attendance, and points can be subtracted for mishaps like forgetting to wear a belt. The students sign an actual contract, understanding that if their point balance falls to zero, they essentially fire themselves from the program. It's a great example of stripping out the emotion.

CHAPTER 39

Count Your Blessings

A Fed survey asked Americans how they would pay for a $400 emergency. The answer: 47 percent of respondents said that they would cover the expense by either borrowing or selling something… or they would not be able to come up with the $400 at all. Four hundred dollars!

⅄ ⅄ ⅄

Advisors are in the *money* business, so it's not surprising they'd spend a good amount of time thinking about money, including their own. Part of our job is to help clients create plans and financial strategies, and we do the same for ourselves, of course. However, it's pretty easy to forget just how blessed we are. To think that nearly 50 percent of Americans would have to borrow or sell something to deal with a $400 unexpected expense is not only surprising but disturbing.

The average US household has annual income of $55,000.[10] It takes $97,000 to be in the top 25 percent of households. And if your income is over $155,000 (congratulations!), you're in the top 10 percent.

A global assessment becomes even more remarkable. A US family earning $100,000 (after taxes) ranks in the richest 2.5 percent of world population, and their income is more than twenty-six times the global average.[11]

So while it makes perfect sense to plan and work hard on your own net worth, it's also helpful to keep in mind just how fortunate we are.

Thoughts

When you think about it, our blessings extend well beyond finances.

- If you have money in the bank and your wallet and spare change in a dish, you're among the top 8 percent of the world's wealthy.
- If you have food in the refrigerator, clothes on your back, and a place to sleep, you are richer than 75 percent in the world.
- If you have never experienced the fear of battle, the loneliness of imprisonment, the agony of torture, or the pangs of starvation, you are more fortunate than seven hundred million people in the world.
- If you can attend church without fear of harassment, arrest, torture, or death, you are more blessed than three billion people in the world.

CHAPTER 40

Thoughtful Spending

Always spend money like
you're in a bear market.
—Larry Helfand (a boss of
mine early in my career)

⅄ ⅄ ⅄

While I absolutely agree with Tom Anderson, my friend and best-selling author of *The Value of Debt*, that debt can serve a meaningful purpose, we're all too familiar with debt amassed for the wrong reasons and the occasionally tragic results. Indeed, there are benefits to leverage when used properly, though debt can serve as a stranglehold and, at times, totally alter one's perspective and course of action.

Let me illustrate the point by sharing a story of something that recently went very wrong for me. I've been an admirer of classic wood boats for some time, and about a year ago, my wife and I made the decision to purchase one if we could find the right vessel. We began our search and checked out a number of beautiful boats, both online and at our lake in Wisconsin. Ultimately, we decided on a stunning 1955 Shepherd with twin engines and looks to kill. Shepherds were made for a limited time in Canada, and we purchased ours from a private party on a lake north of Toronto. The boat was not overly expensive, and it did require some work. A professional performed a survey (examination), and the boat seemed to be in sound condition.

We had it shipped from Canada last fall, and throughout the winter, Lars (I call him the wooden-boat whisperer) and his team worked like artisans on our newly acquired craft. They replaced the interior, added hydraulic steering, and quite simply made the boat look amazing. To my pleasure, we took delivery on a Saturday afternoon during Father's Day weekend, and it's hard to describe just how much enjoyment I had tooling around with my sons, Chris and Danny, for several hours into the early evening.

We decided to get back on the water fairly early Sunday morning, seeking to enjoy a nice cruise before the lake became busy with typical weekend traffic. The boat sank in the first fifteen minutes of our Father's Day cruise.

Saturday Afternoon
Father's Day Weekend

Sunday Morning
Father's Day

To promptly set the record straight, Lars and his team didn't perform work on the boat's bottom, and it had appeared seaworthy when we bought it. Without getting into too much detail, the bottom had a catastrophic failure, which can occur in antique wooden boats. That said, the actual event was chaotic and frightening: the boat sunk quickly, my sons and I had to swim to shore, and our personal items and parts of the boat were scattered everywhere.

As I shared the story ("The boat sank...Yes, everyone is okay...Sure, the boat will be better than ever once repaired") with family and friends over the next few days, people repeatedly told me that they admired how I was handling the misadventure. Friends were genuinely sorry for our loss and sort of blown away that after months of work, it had been delivered Saturday afternoon, only to sink Sunday morning—on, of all days, Father's Day!

I loved searching for the boat, negotiating the deal, deciding what work to have performed, and watching that work being completed over the winter. And as already mentioned, cruising around with my sons was immensely satisfying; family time was one of the primary reasons we had purchased the boat. However, I can tell you that in my heart of hearts, the boat was still just a "thing," and I simply didn't get overly worked up about the mishap. Sure, it stunk, and I wish it wouldn't have happened, but I didn't let it consume me.

So why am I sharing this story, and how does it relate to thoughtful spending? After folks told me that they were amazed at how well I was handling the situation, I started to wonder what enabled me to maintain this grace under pressure. Then it dawned on me that it quite possibly could be that the boat had been a reasonable expenditure, given our net worth and income. How would I react if we had spent ten times the amount we did? (Indeed, there are boats on our lake that cost ten to twenty times more than ours.) What if we were highly leveraged on the boat and overall?

I have to believe that my reaction to our boat's sinking would have been quite different. Everyone likes nice things, but I'm convinced that pointless spending and feeling choked with debt can generate stress that clouds judgment, negatively affecting many other aspects of life.

Thoughts

Life presents enough challenges. Don't purchase more.

CHAPTER 41

Don't Let Money Control You

> For the love of money is a
> root of all kinds of evil.
> —1 Timothy 6:10

⅄ ⅄ ⅄

This is one of the most frequently misquoted verses, and a better understanding can help advisors shape their own perspectives. The misquoted version claims that "money is the root of all evil," implying that money is inherently evil. The accurate version communicates that a "love of money" causes evil. The distinction is important.

If you use money as a measuring stick, relating your self-worth to the size of your bank account, you play a loser's game. There will always be someone with more, and you'll never be content if money is the essence of your identity. For some, financial wealth overshadows the truly important things in life: family, relationships, intellectual stimulation, and so on.

It's easy to see how the love of money, a form of greed, can be the source of many evils.

But money itself doesn't have to be evil at all. Providing for your family, donating to worthy causes, or simply not being a burden to society—all illustrate worthy uses of money. It's paramount to avoid loving or worshiping money in your pursuit of long-term happiness. One helpful practice is to operate under the assumption that you'll be as financially successful as you need to be. How differently would you think or act if you knew you'd have what you need?

Resource

Happy Money: The Science of Smarter Spending, by Elizabeth Dunn and Michael Norton

CHAPTER 42

Life Balance Tactics

> You will never feel truly satisfied by
> work until you are satisfied by life.
> —Heather Schuck

▲ ▲ ▲

This chapter presents varied topics and tactics intended to improve balance in your life.

Lean in. At times, we all face real challenges at work and have to deal with things that aren't fun in the slightest. Let's not confuse these challenges with those addressed in other sections of this book; those previous issues regard not only the futility of maintaining an unsustainable pace but also the times when you simply need to "just say no." Here, I'm referring to tough, unpleasant duties, such as creating a thoughtful and appropriate investment strategy for a client that simply hasn't yet produced results or having to deal with an employee issue when it's the last thing you want to do. As leaders—and especially as ones armed with life plans (see chapter 36)—we can't abdicate our duties. It often helps to view these types of challenges as we would a demanding workout. We're not excited about it, and we probably wish we could be doing something else in those moments, but if we *lean in*, we know our efforts will be rewarded. Don't be addicted to your present feelings.

To what end? A friend told me about a meeting he attended with a supervisor and a colleague. The supervisor had a legitimate criticism, which he raised with his employee. The problem was the boss went on to berate the employee for another fifteen minutes. While it was perfectly appropriate to address the issue, the ensuing rant added no value and, in fact, detracted on all fronts. Besides the employee feeling helpless and frustrated, the supervisor actually reduced the odds of producing solid future performance in his own department. We need to understand that sure, we can take a certain action, perhaps get our pound of flesh, but *to what end*? How does a particular action help someone or even us advance our own objectives?

Be honest and open. We're taught that leaders must always be tough and have all the answers. Given that everyone has weaknesses and that none of us knows everything, I prefer to be candid and openly share some of the challenges I face. Are certain client meetings difficult for you? Are you struggling with an immense volume of work? I'm occasionally candid about various challenges, and I think it fosters a connection with my colleagues and builds credibility.

My "Be Attitudes." Most people have heard of the biblical beatitudes. Well, after assessing some of the happiest individuals I know and recognizing some common traits, I developed my own "be attitudes." And I don't think that anyone can have a true, sustainable joy in his or her life without them.

1. Be Engaged.
2. Be Positive.
3. Be Grateful.
4. Be Soft Hearted.

Don't make a major decision on a "downer." We all have tough days and rough patches. I find it's best to avoid making significant decisions during these times.

The importance of routine. If identifying your goals is an essential first step toward success, establishing supporting routines is a close second. I like to begin each day with the life questions presented in chapter 36. As I'm walking to work and pass a certain area, I make a mental list of the things I'm grateful for that day (you'll always have a few, even on rainy days or when you're not feeling well). I tend to recap a day by counting my successes (again, there are always a few, even on nasty days).

Make your volunteer work easy. Early in my career, when I first began to serve on boards, I was often placed on finance committees, and the work was largely focused on accounting. While I could perform the duties, it's clear that accounting expertise is different from investment expertise, so my participation required meaningful effort. Over the years, I've gravitated toward investment committees and other roles that are integral to my day-to-day activities. If at all possible, try to align your volunteer efforts with your skills in a natural manner.

Continuously learn. A dated survey by the Jenkins Group suggests that 42 percent of college graduates never read another book after college. That strikes me as an unbelievable stat, but even if it's only directionally accurate, it's clear that many adults give up on learning. This is a huge mistake! Thorough documentation has detailed the mental and physical benefits derived from ongoing learning; what's more, having an expanded base of knowledge will help you serve clients, manage employees, raise families, and so on. So whether you do what I did earlier in my career (I would read a book on investments, followed by a book on practice management or self-improvement, then go back to investments, and so on) or take advantage of the many wonderful podcasts, webinars, and more, the benefits of continuous learning are enormous, regardless of the path you choose.

"Just say no" mode. We're all busy, and I think many of us like it that way. But sometimes the pace can border on overwhelming. When I feel stress taking its toll, I give myself permission to enter the "just say no" mode for a month or some appropriate amount of time (determined in advance). This mode gives me permission to say no to pretty much every invite or meeting that's not truly necessary. Of course, saying no rarely applies to clients. But if you really think about it, don't you receive numerous invites that are actually optional? You might not partake in an interesting WebEx, pass on joining your friends at a sporting event, or skip a nice dinner with that portfolio manager who's in town, but freeing up even a handful of hours can really help take the edge off.

Mind, Body and Spirit. I find it important to nurture all three.

Afterword

Growing an advisory practice is quite challenging at times, though it can also be incredibly rewarding on many levels. I'm grateful for the firm my colleagues and I have built, and I'm exceptionally proud of the wide variety of clients we've helped and continue to serve.

Like athletes, artists, and musicians, leaders of advisory practices will never truly master their craft. Things change, and there will always be a need to refine and improve. It's my sincere hope that you embrace and enjoy the journey.

Please feel free to share your experiences, thoughts, and questions. Reach me at www.dimeoschneider.com.

NOTES

1. Valeria Maltoni.

2. Since 2011 including mergers, acquisitions, bankruptcies, plan terminations, etc.

3. Brandon Hall Group study.

4. Bank of Montreal's Wealth Institute April 7, 2015.

5. Advertising Ratios and Budgets Report (Thirty-Ninth Annual).

6. ETF Database, *USA Today*.

7. JP Morgan, David Kelly.

8. JP Morgan—period ending 2015.

9. PGAtour.com—2016 statistics through July 24.

10. CNN Money: 2014 US Central Bureau.

11. www.givingwhatwecan.org: World Bank statistics. Two adults, two children household.

12. Top 50 Consultants ranked by worldwide, institutional tax-exempt advisory assets under advisement as of November 2015; Top 20 Registered Investment Advisors

in 2011, ranked by the most assets added since 2008; Top 10 Consultants by number of reported endowment/foundation consulting clients 2010. Assets as of September 2016.

Also by Bob DiMeo

Nonprofit Asset Management
Effective Investment Strategies and Oversight
Wiley, 2012
With Mathew Rice and Matthew Porter

The Practical Guide to Managing Nonprofit Assets
Wiley, 2005
With William Schneider and Michael Benoit

Asset Management for Endowments & Foundations
Improving Performance & Reducing Management Costs
McGraw-Hill, 1997
With William Schneider and D. Robinson Cluck

Designing a 401(K) Plan
The Hands-On Guide to Creating the
Best Plan for Your Company
Probus Publishing, 1995
With William Schneider

About the Author

From humble beginnings as a straight-commission stockbroker to cofounding and managing the firm *Pensions & Investments* ranks a Top 50 Worldwide Consultant, Bob has embraced a perpetual pursuit to improve and refine his practice. DiMeo Schneider & Associates, L.L.C. advises on over $60 billion in assets and has been recognized as a Top 20 Fastest Growing RIA by *Forbes* and a Top 10 Endowment/ Foundation Consultant by *Plansponsor Magazine.*[12]

Bob has over thirty years of industry experience, and he has co-authored four investment books and numerous articles and whitepapers. He served on the board of directors for IMCA where he chaired the Practice Management effort. Prior to co-founding the firm in 1995, Bob helped lead the institutional consulting effort for Kidder Peabody. He graduated from Bradley University, obtained the CIMA® designation through IMCA's Accreditation Program at the Wharton Business School, and attained a CFP through the College of Financial Planning.

Bob happily serves on the Special Olympics Illinois Foundation Board and the Catholic Charities Investment Committee and Advisory Board. He also mentors for Year Up Chicago. Bob enjoys learning, laughing, golfing, boating, exercising, and spending time with his wife, family, and friends.